The Sunflower

Hanneke Frenken

Written and Illustrated by:
Hanneke Frenken

Translated from Dutch by:
Susanne Chumbley

Published by:
Graviant Publishers, Doetinchem,
The Netherlands

© February 2016

ISBN 978-9491337666

Foreword

Whoever has been to France or Italy probably has seen the big fields with thousands of sunflowers. I love that. The beautiful sunflower is my favourite flower. Every year I plant a sunflower seed in my garden. It is miraculous to see how they germinate and grow. Whenever I went to check on my sunflowers, I noticed that butterflies, bees, ladybirds, bumble bees and other creatures came to visit them. That inspired me to create this book about the sunflower.

I hope you will have a lot of fun reading it.

A small, black and white striped
sunflower seed lay on the ground.

Inside was a baby plant waiting
to come to life.

It started to rain.

After the rain, the sun came out.
The days went past slowly.

The sunflower was given all the nutrition she
needed from the soil, the rain and the sunshine.

One day the sunflower seed opened.

A green little stalk with two small leaves appeared.

The young sunflower was born!

She planted her roots deep and firmly into the soil.

Every day the sunflower grew stronger and bigger.
She grew more leaves and a bud appeared at the top.

The sunflower could hear the wind whisper secrets
from afar.

She could feel the warm kisses of the sun,
and the cool rain showers refreshed her.

Early one morning the bud opened for the very first time.

The sunflower looked around and smiled.

For the first time, she saw other flowers.

She saw the green grass, the trees and the animals.

Whenever she looked up
she saw the blue sky above,
with the clouds and the birds flying past.

"Everything is so beautiful,"
the sunflower thought.

A little mouse with a basket full of berries
walked past.

You could tell by her face that the basket
was heavy, and that she was tired of carrying it.

She sighed and wiped her forehead.

"Hello sunflower," said the mouse.

"I picked a basket full of berries
that I have to take home.

The basket is too heavy to carry.

Can I hide some berries between your roots?

I will come and collect them later."

The sunflower heard what the mouse
asked her and smiled.

The mouse dug a little hole
and buried three berries.

After the mouse had left a butterfly
landed on the sunflower.

"What a beautiful colours does that
butterfly have,"
the sunflower thought.

The butterfly waved.

"Hello, sunflower.

I have been flying the whole day.

You have strong big leaves.

Can I sit on them and have a rest?"

The sunflower smiled.

She loved the company of the beautiful butterfly.

The butterfly chose a leaf and sat down.

A busy honey bee
had also seen the sunflower.

"Hi sunflower," said the bee.

"I heard that you have lovely honey.

Can I come over and eat some?"

The sunflower smiled.

Of course, would she let this happy bee
eat from her honey.

The bee flew to the middle of the sunflower,
and tasted the honey.

"Yum, that tastes lovely," he hummed.

After Spring came Summer.

The sun, that had warmed her so nicely
before,
spread a burning heat.

The rain didn't come and the soil dried out.

There was not a drop of water to be found.

The sunflower was so thirsty.

"I have to drink," she thought.

But she couldn't drink.

In the end, her little head dropped down.

The little mouse was just on her way to the sunflower for a little chat.

When she saw the sunflower she was shocked.

"This is not good," she thought.

"Our sunflower is in danger!

I have to go and get help!"

The sunflower felt more and more unwell.

The little mouse ran as fast as she could
to a stream, and filled her basket with water
so the sunflower could have a drink.

The butterfly waved her wings to make a cool
breeze to cool the sunflower down, and the
honeybee was humming songs to cheer her up.

The sunflower tried to smile
when she saw how everyone
tried to help her so lovingly.

The sun burned hotter.

Then she couldn't do it anymore.

The sunflower smiled one last time
and closed her eyes.

The moon stood high in the
dark, starry sky.

It wasn't as warm as
in the afternoon.

The mouse, the butterfly
and the honeybee were
kneeling down next to
the sunflower.

"Our beautiful, sweet flower is dead,"
sobbed the bee.

"She has always looked after us.
I am going to miss her."

"I am going to miss her too,"
answered the mouse.

The butterfly nodded.

They were quiet for a
moment.

Then the mouse pointed at something
that was lying on the ground.

"Have a look at this.
There are all black and white striped
things lying here," she said.

"Those are sunflower seeds,"
said the butterfly.

"Next year a new sunflower will
be growing here again."

About this book

This book shows children how a big, strong sunflower grows from a little seed, and how the sunflower's life goes.

The sunflower makes friends with a mouse, a butterfly and a honey bee. Clear illustrations support the story.

The story is simple but has a poetic edge to it.